THE THREE-TOED SLOTH
AND OTHER TALES

Scott Melville

Copyright © 2018 Scott Melville
All rights reserved.

As always, to Julie

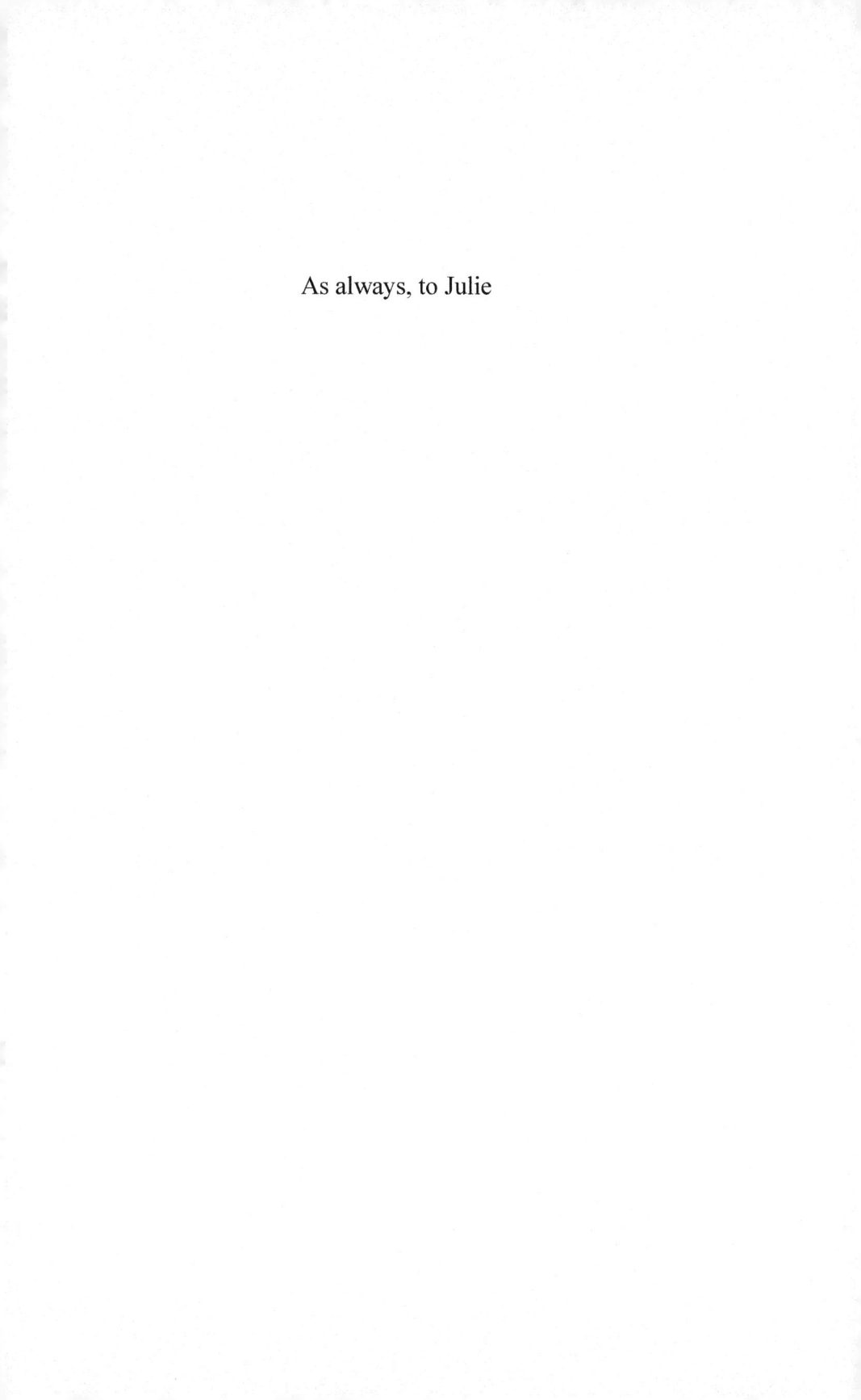

BOOKS BY SCOTT MELVILLE

TEXTBOOKS
The Science of Coaching Tennis
Teaching Elementary Health and Physical Education: A
      Guide for Classroom Teachers
Health and Fitness: An Elementary Teacher's Guide

EDITED POETRY
Landscape Lovers, Lords of Language: Poetic Thoughts on
      Nature
The Scent of These Armpits: Poetic Thoughts on Sport

POETRY
Prose Poems of an Exercised, Socialistic, Vegetarian,
      Tree-Hugging Freethinker
More Poems of an Exercised, Socialistic, Vegetarian,
      Tree-Hugging Freethinker
My Poetry: Such As It Is
Here a Moo, There a Moo
How's Retirement?
Quiet Limb Time
Libations
This Dust of Thought
Single-Speed Time
Inviting My Soul
Leavings
Left Back in Camp
Close to Home
Short Poems
When Dogs Chased Cars
Back of the Barn
Byways

Tutta Una Famiglia (a collection of my baseball poems)
The Three-Toed Sloth and Other Tales

CONTENTS

Preface	ix
Radiating	1
Athletic License	2
Deciphering a Poem	3
Dad and Our Family Fishing Trips	4
Beach House Not On the Beach (Newport, CA)	6
Guilty Pleasure	8
The Names We Give Them	9
K-T Event	10
Little Lime Green Frog	11
Flashbacks	12
Small Town Gardening	13
Entomological Facts	14
Small Town Gardening	15
The Three-Toed Sloth	16
Childhood Downpours	17
Toto and Tricky Woo	18
Playing Ball, Stick, and Frisbee	20
My Charismatic Talk on Bugs	22
Note from Your Great Uncle Scott	24
Our United Methodist Church	26
Camping Out In the Early Permian Period	28
A Barn of Good Character That I've Sketched in Different Weather	29
Bad Back	30
All Men and Women Hate Me	31
Imbalance	32
At Ease	33
Commemorating the Pencil and the Attached Eraser	34

Fundamentals	36
We Rent Goats	38
Giving Your Three Cents	39
The Howdy Doody Show	40
Turning Two	41
The Original Unflipped NASA Image AS17-148-22727	42
Community Poolside Party, Fourth of July, 2018	44
The Crossing	46
Being Served	48
From Haunts of Coot and Hern	49
Upon Examination of My One-Wood	50
Sand	52
Blue	54
Competitive Freediver	55
All-Embracing Supplication	56
The Coming of the End Times -- Civilization As We Know It	57
Precisely At Sunset	58
Smash-Mouth Pickleball	59
All the Marbles	60
Thrill Riding and Graceful Dismounts	61
One Big Ass Sparkly Pinwheel	62
Upper Paleolithic Man	64
Dunkirk	65
About the Author	67

PREFACE

Here's my eighteenth book of poetry. These fifty poems were completed May 2018 through September 2018.

The image on the front cover is from my painting *Three-Toed Sloth* (8.25"x14").

Eighteen books of 50 poems each adds up to 900. That's about half as many as Dickinson wrote. She got a lot earlier start than me, but died when she was 56. I wrote my first poem when I was 64. That was six years ago. I'm estimating that I've sat down and cudgeled the old bean an average of at least 3 hours a day (discounting moments of fiddling with my tea or aimlessly picking my nose). That means I've put in around six and a half thousand hours. There's this *10,000 Hour Rule* which says that in order to achieve your peak performance in most any endeavor (sports, the arts and such) you must have had a good solid 10,000 hours of practice. I would like to take this to mean that there are better poems in my future. But of course, I have to worry about how well the already rickety synapses, the rotting overhead rafters, will hold up. Also, every time I complete a poem, I have the fear that I'll not be able to think of one more thing to write about -- that that one was my last, and I'm left utterly empty.

Radiating

*Color makes its impact from contrasts
rather than from its inherent qualities.*
-- Claude Monet

Look Jane, Look!
that red bird in the green grass,
bold breasted, bursting,
such a clash, collision of primary colors
crying out loud.

That hot red spot, that expanse
of cool spring green,
opposite sides of the spectrum
tingling with excitement,
duking it out, wonderfully at war.

This sight shouldn't work, it seems
slapped together, borders
on the gimmick, the razzle-dazzle,
the glitzy.

Besieged, delighted, my receptors
need time to recover,
my cones must calm down,
collect themselves.

Athletic License

On a classic 4 to 6 to 3 double play
the shortstop doesn't deign to brush the bag
as he takes the toss and flicks the throw,
he knows he's close enough to get the call,
glides past with a certain élan,
eludes the slider with a practiced panache.

Is there an artist or poet,
in box seat or beyond centerfield,
who'd not applaud, approve,
rise up and cheer the disregard,
the slick bending of the rule?

Deciphering a Poem

I like things I like without having to work at liking them,
things that come already assembled.
Is that such a shortcoming? such a crime?
It doesn't mean I don't like learning new things,
seeing things in new ways, stumbling upon new thoughts,
or finding old ones deep in a drawer.

Maybe I would understand this person's poem,
or like the gymnastics of it, if I tried harder, if I read
it yet again, looked up this and that word.
I've done most all the things Billy Collins recommends,
held it up to the light, pressed my ear to its hive,
tried waterskiing across it.
I've taken the book firmly in both hand, put my nose
within an inch of the page and stared at it
as if it were a magic eye image, squinted, slowly
moved it in and out, let my eyes lose focus and go fuzzy,
and still was left with a bunch of jiggly lines.

Dad and Our Family Fishing Trips

Dad finished ninth grade and then took care of the farm.
After the war, he worked at a factory that made
brake-shoes for the railroads. He put in a lot of overtime.
For as long as I can remember as a kid, other than
Christmas Day, New Years, the 4th of July,
and Labor Day, he got one week of vacation.

The car would be all packed and we'd get up
and leave at two o'clock in the morning.
It was a 10 or 12 hour drive up into Ontario on mostly
two-lane roads. We stopped and fixed a roadside
breakfast along the way: eggs, bacon, and orange juice.

Our plywood cabin huddled in birch trees next to a lake;
there was a wood stove, a sink and cold water faucet,
a bare lightbulb in the rafters, a table with chairs around it,
a cupboard of pots and faded plastic plates,
a drawer of heavy silverware.
We shared a few sagging beds and a single outhouse.

We swam, boated, caught, cleaned and ate
pickerel and norther pike, fashioned an old board
into a water ski and tried to get up --
the Evinrude outboard gurgled and smoked,
half managed to keep our skinny bodies out of the water.
In the evenings or early mornings everyone took turns
washing in the lake with a bar of ivory soap,
Joel and I did it together.

Each afternoon Dad liked to sit in a lawn chair
and snooze on the beach. I recall how white his legs were
in the bright sun. One shin was badly deformed,
a pulley had fallen on it at work, doctors didn't know
if it could be saved.

One particular day, on the last of our summer trips,
I remember him squinting into the sun and watching
the head of a black dog out in the middle of the lake.
The dog would swim toward a white bobbing flock
of seagulls. When he got close they took off,
circled around and landed on another side of the lake.
The dog turned and made the long journey
in that direction, patiently paddled with straining neck,
and again the birds rose and settled elsewhere,
again and again.

Dad turned to me and said, "Well by gad,
would you look at that," and gave me
his light blue-eyed sparkle, his ho ho chuckle.

Beach House Not On the Beach (Newport Beach, CA)

It's crammed into the community,
pushed up against the car-lined street,
hard against a single-lane sidewalk,
separated from its peers by a shoulder-squeezing
passageway on one side, a tunneled slit
for bicycles and garbage cans on the other.

The rooms are clogged with furniture:
rustic, distressed. There are narrow stairs
and hallways. A slow turning ceiling fan
tries to circulate the confined air.
Carved masks and paintings of seashores
and sailing ships crowd the walls.
Goo haws abound: seashells, bowls
of smooth rounded stones,
surfing figurines, coral sculptures.

The patio in back is a confusion
of driftwood, pots and plants.
Strange flourishing cacti, succulents, nameless
blooming things squat and spread,
cling and entwine, curl and exclaim.

And the wind chimes of every wooden sort,
here and there, and elsewhere,
gently bump in the breeze.

The soft hollow clicks confirm, enunciate,
that all, all this crowded hodgepodge,
this confined mishmash of discordant stuff,
bestows casualness, consonance.
It works, adds up, is funky good.

Guilty Pleasure

Left alone and unsupervised
I put a baking potato, the biggest I can find,
in the microwave.
While it's humming and revolving in there,
I open a can of baked beans.
I use an old fashion opener
that you have to crank. I prefer it that way.
I feel cowboy-ish, think of being on the range,
that the day has been long and hard,
I'm next the fire and the chuckwagon.

When the potato is done and piping hot,
I slice it up on a plate and mash it down
with a fork. The steam rises to my face
and I take in the down-to-earth smell of tuber.

Then I plop the beans on top.
I eat it all, leave no skin, get every last bean.
Although I'm a vegetarian, I save
the little square of pork fat for the last bite,
roll it on my tongue and squish into it,
take in its succulence.

The Names We Give Them

cats have kittens
dogs have pups

cows have calves
horses have colts

sheep have lambs
bears have cubs

kangaroos have joeys
chickens have chicks

geese have goslings
frogs have polliwogs

octopi have fry
foxes have kits

platypuses have puggles
pigs have piglets

owls have owlets
swans have cygnets

sloths have baby sloths
gorillas have infants

K-T Event

What is so rare as a day in June?
Then, if ever, come perfect days;
Then heaven tries earth if it be in tune,
and over it softly her warm ear lays;
Whether we look, or whether we listen,
We hear life murmur, or see it glisten.
-- James Russell Lowell

It happened in June, so the scientists say,
so the buried pollen samples say.
A far-flung iron rock, 6 miles wide,
barreled in at 10 to 20 miles per second,
the blast 7 billion times greater than Hiroshima,
the crater 110 miles wide, 12 miles deep --
through the crust, towards the warm core --
a bullet in the belly.

Glowing fireballs, sulfurous ash
spewed up, rained down,
burnt the earth and blotted the sun.
Giants gasped, rotted in the valleys, on the hills
and plains, bobbed in the ocean waves
and slowly sank.

Stench in place of fragrance,
black and dun in place of blue and green.
An ordered, thriving world, gone in a swipe,
a swat, gone in a blink of an eon's eye,
never again to be heard or seen.

Little Lime Green Frog

I arise early to work in my study.
I like to have the windows open
for the fresh air and bird vanguard.
Until today, for a solid two months,
a small frog has been out there
in the still dark, in the flower bed.
His call is not deep enough
to be called a croak, but it's clear,
more than a grating click, much more
than any cricket could manage.

He croaks, or whatever, for as many
as 16 or 17 times in consistent frog rhythm,
and then usually waits it out for minutes.
Sometimes it has been effective in
eliciting a response from the far side
of the house. A delayed back and forth
Morse Code like messaging comes
into play.

I can't see the little bugger, but
surely he's in his crouched seated position,
throat pulsing. He's got his smug look,
his big liquid eyes, his little fingers
splayed.

I miss him.
 I'm worried about him.

Flashbacks

Some 60 years ago, through an underwater
viewing window, I watched a mama hippo
and her baby. The baby was zooming
down and around, doing loop-de-loops,
a little pink square with rounded corners.
He could go and go for the longest time
without surfacing, hippo paddling away,
emitting little streams of bubbles.
I might not think of him for years and then
there he is, as acrobatic, as energetic,
as joyful as ever, maybe even more
exuberant.

I remember seeing an old Bonny and Clyde
movie where one of the bank robbing clan
had been shot in the head. The FBI agents
were standing around with their guns
watching the man's last moments.
He was crawling about and incoherently
talking of his old hound dog and how it
had eaten someone's shoe or something like that.

You never know what your last hours could be like,
if you might be lucid or losing it -- babbling away.
I can see my old self with dazed look,
coming out with something along the lines of,
"Look at the little hippo go!
Look at him go!"

Small Town Gardening

Mom and Dad believed that you
worked first and then you could play.
One of my chores was helping in the garden.
Back then, instead of lawns,
most of the folks had good sized gardens
which pretty much ran from the back
of the house out to the alley.

I remember tapping the stakes into the ground,
tightening the binder twine to mark off straight rows,
making a shallow furrow with the edge of my hoe,
and Dad's instructions to drop in three corn seeds
at 12 inch intervals.

I remember pushing the cultivator up
and down the rows, getting down
and pulling the weeds from around onions,
lettuce, tomatoes, carrots and cucumbers.
I can see those low-lying weeds
with their thick red stems, and what their
roots looked like after they had given way.

I remember sitting at our white picnic table
with Mom, snapping the ends off the string beans
and tossing them into a pan of water,
husking the corn, setting aside some tender ones
to have for lunch.

Entomological Facts

I'm happy to meet a praying mantis in the grass,
a grand daddy long legs on the side of the house,
a caterpillar deliberately crossing the walk.
It's fun to discover a walking stick holding still,
and investigate his thinness.
I like to hear cicadas high up in the summer trees,
evening crickets and katydids defining the night.
It's interesting seeing a measuring worm doing its thing,
a spider stringing her web, centipedes
scurrying out from under an overturned rock.
It makes me smile to touch a roly-poly, or have
a ladybug land on my shoulder and dwell for a bit.
There can't be too many slow flying fireflies
in the June dusk, or too many butterflies flouncing
or sunning themselves in the flower beds
(whatever color is fine, a-okay with me).

But you don't want to find streams of ants
going from the cupboard to the sink,
a hive of wasps directly over the backdoor,
a bunch of fleas hopping off of anything
(no matter how impressive their leaps).
It's never good to have locus or grasshoppers
darkening the sky, gnawing on the fenceposts.
One Japanese beetle on a tomato plant is too many,
one cockroach on the kitchen floor with twitching feelers,
one horsefly on your neck, a housefly preening
on your plate, a long-neck stinkbug slow walking
on your pillow, a midge on your leg, a louse

in your hair, a bloated tick on your chest
or under your arm, a mosquito playing a violin
next your ear, a hairy scorpion spending the night
in your shoe, or a black beetle falling on your collar
and tumbling down your back.

The Three-Toed Sloth

Hanging upside down in the tropical rainforest canopy,
eating a certain sort of leaf: slow metabolism,
little muscle, more gut than anything else.
Snoozing 15 hours a day, traveling 41 yards at most.
Inching down once a week to the forest floor to poop.

His long hair, coated with fungus, wild green in color,
perfect camouflage, a place for resident insect species,
the fluttering lifecycle of moths.

Mute professor of calm deliberateness,
conservation, symbiosis.

Childhood Downpours

There'd come the sudden mad pounding on the roof,
the hissing, splashing liquidity of sounds.
We ran to the windows front and back,
looked through rivulets and took in the translucent
world. It was alive with the splashing jiggling dance
of water on road and roof, puddle and pool.
The gutters were swirling, gushing, overflowing.

And when it subsided and passed, the soaked trunks
of the maples stood black, the lower limbs
bowed almost to the ground as if in thanks.
The green green leaves hung limp, exhausted.
Trickles and drips amplified the quiet.
The expanse of lawn was transformed
into a shallow silver lake, clothesline poles
protruded from the surface, their drooping ropes
a row of clinging drops.

Gathering ourselves, we wondered how the beans
and flowers fared, if the upstairs ceiling had leaked,
if there was water in the basement, and if we should
go see whether or not the sump-pump had kicked on.

Toto and Tricky Woo

For as long as I can remember,
wherever I have lived and met new friends,
and had them over to the house,
the women (all those without children
or whose children have grown and gone)
will say, "Your paintings are wonderful.
Are you in a gallery? You should sell them.
Would you paint my dog?"

So here I am with a glossy 3 x 5 mug shot
of two Pomeranians. They're staring straight at me
with their black bulging eyes, their black noses.
One is showing a hint of pink tongue.
They are all fluffed up, have as much contrast
and texture as you could find in Minnie
and Micky Mouse.

Their loving owner doesn't know
that I don't like little dogs: Toy Terriers,
Pugs, Pekingese, Poodles, Shih Tzus,
Chihuahuas, Miniature Schnauzers and such.
I have a coyote-like contempt for them,
think of them as weak, subservient, over-cuddled,
coddled. I've never been comfortable
with their quivering nervousness, their locks
and bows, their tiny outfits to keep them warm.
I don't like their piercing yaps,
to hear their tiny feet scratching across the floor,

their bothersome whimpering to be let in or out,
the little puddles and presents they leave.

I'll do my best,
I'll do my level best to create a pretty picture
of the darling pair, to capture the innocent look,
to strive for cuteness, seek the syrupy,
and avoid dropping a sinister gleam
into those liquid eyes.

Playing Ball, Stick, and Frisbee

These are elemental games of chase and retrieve,
good exercise and excellent bonding activities.
They can be played most anywhere,
in most weather conditions. They can consist
of a couple of throws or a great number
depending on the time you have available.
The equipment is simple and inexpensive.

You should always go all out, running after
the implement as fast as you can, try
to catch the ball when it's still bouncing.
Go up after the frisbee, be fully airborne if possible,
maybe throwing in some sort of swivel hips move.

You should bring the tossed object directly back
to the thrower at a good trot, head up.

The same concept applies if a body of water
is involved. Paddle vigorously out to get it
and return snortingly to shore, as directly
as the current permits.

It's ok to shake off water next to the thrower,
it fits the lighthearted laughing, tail-wagging
spirit of the game and should be expected.

Always readily relinquish the object;
tug of war wresting is an entirely different sport
with its own merits, head shaking and growling criteria.

Engaging in it here interrupts the back and forth
flow of the game.

The thrower should give "atta boys,"
and "good dogs." Although they are not needed
they are always welcome. Treats are unnecessary
and could serve to undermine intrinsic motivation.

Playing on ice or other slipper surfaces
can be entertaining for the thrower
but somewhat frustrating for the retriever
and should not be overdone.

Flinging devices can be purchased and used
to achieve further throws, but it does introduce
an imbalance in effort and raises the issue
of full and fair commitment.

Faints, fake throws and hiding of the object
behind the back is contraindicated under
all circumstances, it is considered poor sportsmanship
and has no place in the game.

Nor should waterlogged sticks ever be thrown,
careless or otherwise.

Finally, if the implement is lost in the grass
the thrower should immediately go get it
and restart the game from that spot. Standing,
pointing and shouting "over there" is always ineffectual
and shows weak mindedness on the part of the thrower.

My Charismatic Talk on Bugs

*I turned a grey stone over: a hundred forky-tails
seethed from under it like thoughts out of an evil mind.
-- George Mackay Brown (*Fine Green Waves*)*

At a family get together, I happened
to be eating at the younger folk's table.
There were four of them,
high school and college aged,
and I was smack dab in the middle.
Nothing was being said, some were
looking at their phones between bites.
After a while it seemed to me
that something should be said.
I blurted out, "there's a lot fewer
insects around now days."
They all looked at me.
I felt I needed to elaborate.
"When I was young, if you were sitting
or lying in the grass, there would be
walking sticks, granddaddy longlegs,
praying mantises, lady bugs,
all kinds of strange critters jumping,
crawling, buzzing or fluttering by.
Or when you turned over a rock
there would be a mass of slithering
squirming centipedes and such,
a mad dash of scurrying beetles and spiders."
They remained speechless,
so I forged ahead, tried to bolster my thesis.

"When you were out at night
there would be swarms of moths
and whirling things about the streetlights.
If you were driving down the road
with the high beams on, it could look
like your were going through a snowstorm.
They would be smacking into your windshield,
leaving streaking splatters big and small,
green and yellow. I remember oohing over
the thwacks of some of the June Bugs."
Silence still reigned, they were looking down
or at one another with half smiles.
I sat there for a bit longer, decided against
hypothesizing, delving into pesticides,
loss of hedgerows, uni-crop fields,
light pollution, global warming.
I announced I was going to get
a piece of cake, and left them in peace.

Note from Your Great Uncle Scott

I remember, I remember, the house where I was born,
The little window where the light can peeping in at morn...
-- Thomas Hood

I doubt that you will find anything of interest in my stuff.
All these shelves and stacks of toppling books.
I don't expect that you'll have a place for them,
or that they're the sort you'll want to read.
You might wonder about this old Roy Roger's alarm clock.
You could probably get a couple of hundred bucks for it
on eBay. It still works.

It used to sit on the window sill of the bedroom
your grandfather and I shared. His bed was tucked under
the sloping roof on one side, mine under the other.
I don't remember it ever having been set to wake us up
in the morning. Your great great grandmother
did that on rainy and snowy days. She would sing
up the stairs, "Time to rise and shine! Joeli Olli!
Scoot Scoot Scooter! Scooter Rizooter! Time for school!"
More often that not the sun, all by itself, would do
the stirring. The window faced east, the golden light
flooded in, eddied and swirled about the ceiling, walls,
our tousled hair, filled our sleepy eyes.
Looking out across the street, through the limbs
of the big maple trees, there was an open lot
between Grinnel's house and old lady Floyd's.
That's where we played ball.
Your granddad was five years older than me.

He taught me how to play. He pitched to me underhand,
laid it right in my wheelhouse, met my bat.
He threw balls so that I had to run and catch them,
led me just right, forehand and backhand,
threw them high over my head until I could go straight
back and make over the shoulder catches like Willy Mays.
I ran my heart out. I loved it,
and loved him.

Our United Methodist Church

It sat at the end of the block, six houses away,
red brick secure, modest. The street was lined with
thick girthed maple trees, the bark rough and curling,
the sidewalks raised up in many places by their roots.

I went with my hair parted and slicked down. I wore
a light gray suit, a narrow clip on tie with subdued stripes,
a starchy plain white shirt with cufflinks, and black dress
shoes. It was important to keep the shoes polished.
We had a shoe box at home. It was wooden, painted red.
I remember the round shallow tin of polishing wax,
the smell of the polishing rag, the soft bristled brush
for buffing.

I never learned all that much about the church's doctrine.
John Wesley was the founder. We were strong believers
in all rising and singing a lot of hymns. The cross
on the altar was empty because Christ had arisen.
We didn't have him still stuck up there
like the Catholics did.

Each summer we would have an ice cream social.
Folding tables with white sheets, and folding wooden
chairs were set up in the front lawn. Mom would
give me a quarter to put in the cup. Dad was always
down in the basement with his strong hands,
assigned the task of digging in and dishing up
the vanilla ice cream. He gave all the kids super

big scoops. I remember the cake to be squarely cut,
white with white frosting.

The church might have had other fund raisers but
I don't remember them. We didn't believe in gambling
and playing bingo like the Catholics did. But I know
Dad was always betting on the baseball games at work.
If the team he picked ever got 13 runs in a game
he would win big time.

Since those days a number of the old maples have died,
their stumps removed, the sidewalks smoothed out.
A big new wing has been added to the building,
the next-door parsonage has been removed to make way
for a paved parking lot in back and around the side.
The great wooden front doors have been replaced
with glass ones. All these things seem like serial
desecrations to me.

Camping Out In the Early Permian Period

The swamp's day turns to warm sticky evening,
the air heavy -- insufferably laden with oxygen,
no bird sings, there are no birds.
Giant bugs buzz, clatter, squirm, slither, scurry,
brashly march about as if they owned the place,
congregate and swarm together as they please.

Dragonflies as big as seagulls come over,
hover and dart away. There are eight-foot long
millipedes, cockroaches that could take on a cat,
hairy bodied spiders, glossy armored beetles,
dysmorphic arthropods with spikes and claws,
cleaving mandibles, giant things with bulging
multiple eyes and long twitching feelers.

The sun sets red. I push my stakes
into the yielding humus, crawl into my tent
and zip the zipper, lie back and stare up,
take in the dark's pulsing clicks and clacks,
its revving clamber. Something heavy
thuds upon the canvas, inches from my face,
chooses to reside there, then another comes,
and another.

A Barn of Good Character That I've Sketched in Different Weather

There's this abandoned wooden barn I know,
that sits alone on a tilted field, on rather rocky ground.
It's modest, rectangular, has a cupola set somewhat
forward of center. The cupola is dual gabled,
louvered on all four sides.

I wonder about the man who built it,
what help he might have had, what dreams,
how much it set him back, if it was most all he had.
And about that cupola, and how it came to be
a bit more ornate than ventilation would decree.

Bad Back

The mature muscular man,
lithe, firm-fibered, upright
with expansive lungs,
exhaling health, full of pride,
exemplar of action and stir,
faithful exponent of movement,
apostle of work and vigorous play,
sturdy believer,

laid low, laid up, brought down,
curtailed, cribbed, confined,
beset with the dull,
the sharp dash and dart of pain,
with the angst of inactivity,
with hedged prognoses,
the specter of shuffling
and propped up prospects.

All Men and Women Hate Me

I am the rat.
I lead my life, I feed my young.
I am discrete, I keep from sight, come out at night,
you might hear me overhead or in the walls.
If you should see me, there are more,
or so the adage goes.

You shout and shriek,
say I'm big and fat, exaggerate my size,
claim I carry fleas, spread disease,
contract out to have me trapped,
there's nothing worst than a rotting rat.

Imbalance

There can be too many people on the streets
and roads, on the beaches, in the campgrounds
and on the hiking trails; too many living in the valleys,
ringing the hillsides and ridges, sprawled out
through the countryside, or crammed on top
of each other next to train tracks, freeways
and power plants.

There can be too many people gathered
outside seven-elevens or closing bars,
too many sleeping in the parks with packs,
too many in prison yards and detention centers,
too many trekking across borders, trying
to scale fences or fleeing in overloaded boats.

There can be too few people in dusty dying towns,
in city neighborhoods with crumbling walks;
there can be one too few in a creaking house,
across a table, or in a bed.

At Ease

I went to the beach at sunset,
got up on a ledge, was set for formal splendor,
expected golden garb, frills, glint and trailing
tassels, a fireball wrapped in warm scarves,
coordinated robes of rose and purple,
mellow luster, the water all sequins and sheen.

I caught her stretched out, lounging,
ready to turn in, shorn of brocades
and embroidery, lace and shimmering jewels.
Colorless, featureless clouds clung,
smudged out the sun and clad the pale
gray line of sea.

And I was okay with the plain, the casual,
the carelessness, okay without all the
accouterments, the makeup, liner and rouge.

Commemorating the Pencil and the Attached Eraser

March 30th is National Pencil Day

My primary school classroom had one of those old
pencil sharpeners sitting up front, firmly screwed
to the windowsill. Without asking permission,
we could get up and sharpen our pencils anytime
we wanted, rigorously crank away, loudly grind
them down to a perfect point.
I've always liked pencils, liked to start the new year,
each new day with a newly sharpened one, or better yet,
with a fistful. I would return to my desk renewed,
determined to do better, to outperform myself.

The smell of a fresh shaved one, the love of it,
has stayed with me. And I've never been comfortable
reading a book without one in my forefingers,
even if I'm not taking notes or underlining anything.

I've read that a single pencil can draw a line
35-miles long, or write around 45,000 words.
It was Hymen Lipman, in 1858, who came up
with the idea of attaching an eraser on the end.
The U.S. Supreme Court ruled that it wasn't
really an invention. They said that both the pencil
and the eraser were known technologies,
and combining the two was only an innovation.

I guess I concur with that ruling and approve
of the idea of others being able to copy his idea
and make it pretty much universal (except for golf pencils).
Nevertheless I see it as a landmark innovation.

I could better revere a statue of Hymen
in the town square than I could of some Civil War general
who lead men into battle and left havoc in his path.
Those military statues can be pretty dramatic
with rearing warhorses and unsheathed sabers.
Hymen had a flowing beard which is always good.
I would have him bigger than life, high up on a pedestal,
precariously tipped back in a chair, his feet on an old
rustic desk. He would be gazing up as though thinking,
There'd be an eraser-less pencil behind his ear or
crossways in this mouth, maybe one of his hands
would be stroking his bead, the other poised as though
drumming the desktop.

Fundamentals

In my beginning is my end. -- T.S. Eliot

In small gyms, on playgrounds grassy and paved,
I taught children all eight of the locomotor skills,
the building blocks of movement: walking,
running jumping, leaping, sliding, galloping,
hopping, skipping. I led them up and down, fast and slow,
high and low, forwards and backwards, stepped on the lines
and avoided them. We did bear walks and bunny hops,
were frogs and kangaroos, lumbered like elephants,
whinnied and galloped like wild horses let loose.

I taught the non-locomotor skills of bending, curling,
stretching, balancing, swinging, twisting. We were
tall trees swaying in the breeze. We scrunched down low
like turtles, drooped like flowers in need of rain, rose up
like the sun, balanced like ballerinas and flamingoes,
twirled like tops and whirling dervishes.

I taught the developmental manipulative skills: throwing,
kicking, striking, dribbling. I dressed them in games
galore, set out the cones, created the rules and goals,
brought out balloons and playground balls.
And there was shouting and cheers between
the ringing of the bells.

Now at 70, I've returned to the rudimentary motions,
the elemental core. Walking is my only mode,
my scope and stride is shortened. I no longer twist

or torque or do the dervish stuff.
And I've taken up a simple, less whizzing game, share
a smaller court, swing at plastic balls with shorten paddles,
take more compacted strokes. The glee is softened,
the frolic more subdued, the fun, the fundamental
childish fun -- it's still strong, still there.

We Rent Goats

For their logo, they've got a good pen and ink
portrait of a goat in profile. There's the twisting
horns, the flowing goatee and mane.
He's got that smug haughty look that patriarchal
goats can have.

Their mottos are:
You name it, the goats can clear it,
and, *Will work for food.*

No terrain is too steep, too tough,
they'll eat anything from the top down,
seeds and all. Other than cactus, stinging nettle
and tumble weed, nothing is too noxious.
Just turn us loose, 100 goats, a half acre a day.

And they've got those bright-eyed
black and white work-loving dogs:
Atty, Andy, Rowdy, Jo Jo.
Sid passed away from cancer in 2010,
is buried next to the home pen --
though not moving well, she worked
the goats to the end.

Giving Your Three Cents

Writing is the practice of thinking before you speak,
before you open your gob and blurt out something stupid.
You listen to yourself, ask if it makes sense, if it's
understandable, if it's interesting, if it's truly true.
You consider whether or not you're slurring your words,
mumbling, babbling, cackling, if you should say it
from a different view. Or if you should just zip it,
 shut up and put a cork in it.

The Howdy Doody Show

It was the only program on tv for me,
a half hour on Saturday mornings.
Buffalo Bob's grinning face leaned
in close to the stage.
Howdy, in his plaid shirt, pranced
on a maze of white strings,
his eyelids and jaw being worked up and down,
his arms and legs jerked about.

How I sat close before the screen,
waited out the network's off-the-air signal,
sang along, took it all in.
Now I wonder if Bob might have been
a child molester or some such thing
in his spare time,
or if when the camera stopped
he didn't say something like, "There,
that ought to hold the little bastards."

Turning Two

I'm amazed when I hear others crossover
and break into a foreign language,
nod and laugh about it as if it were nothing.
It reminds me how parochial I am,
makes me feel like a bumpkin, a hayseed,
how bush-league I am.

I marvel at their fluidity,
how their mouths make different sounds,
how they field the ball, scoop it up
and flick it around,
Tinkers to Evers to Chance.

The Original Unflipped NASA Image AS17-148-22727

*When asked about Western Scotland,
Samuel Johnson replied, "Worth seeing,
but not worth going to see."*

I'm not into space travel.
I don't want to put on a pressurized suit,
squeeze into a nosecone,
have to check this and that,
fiddle with a bunch of dials,
and then be blasted off into space,
my head pushed back against the seat,
my face contorted into a grimace,
go 18,000 miles straight up,
turn around with the sun behind me
to see where I came from.

But this picture Jack Schmitt took
in December, 1972 was done
with a steady hand, is mighty good,
mighty clean. The old place does indeed
look like a glowing blue marble,
made of glass, hanging out there
in the black with its white whirls
and modest green and brown patches.

Although it's disorienting to see
Antarctica up at the top and north Africa

and Saudi Arabia upside down,
I find myself saying, "Ah yes, Antarctica
would be catching sun at this time of year."
And, "Yes, of course, those desert places
would be cloudless, wouldn't they."

I understand that that sweet swirl
in the top right had a darker side,
was a cyclone that brought high winds
and flooding to more than one Indian soul.
From here it all looks so still, so serene,
delicate and dainty.

Talk about an image drawing you in,
speaking to you, making you want to go there.

Community Poolside Party, Fourth of July, 2018

The kids are dunking and splashing,
screaming and squealing, tossing a ball.
The parents are busily attending to the food.
One heavyset father is out in the middle
letting his skinny daughter climb up his back,
stand on his shoulders and leap off,
holding her nose.

I sit in the shade with the old.
It's pleasant, but I don't particularly enjoy
small talking with people I've just met
or hardly know. I suspect more than half of them
believe that President Trump is doing a good job,
or haven't even thought about it.

It is interesting to think of the role I now play,
Shakespeare's sixth act, in shorts
with shrunk shank. I think about how
I got here, this time and place so far
from where I started.

I had never been near a swimming pool
when I was young. Joel and I would
take towels and walk through the burdock
and cow patties of Giles' pasture,
there was the muddy banks of the creek,
we jumped off the thick limb of the leaning willow.

My one recollection of the 4th
was up at Gramma's farm.
I ran about the yard swirling a sparkler,
was fascinated with the streaming afterglow,
and how black it was when it fizzled out.

I don't have the least desire to set off a cherry bomb
or stay up tonight to watch the fireworks.
I look forward to going home,
being home with Julie.

The Crossing

If I can stop one heart from breaking,
I shall not live in vain,
If I can ease one life the aching,
Or cool one pain,
Or help one fainting robin
Unto his nest again,
I shall not live in vain.
-- Emily Dickinson

She came, out of nowhere, out of
the deep grass, straight across the street
with her toddling string of fuzzy ducklings,
15 or 20 at least. She was proud, stoic,
yellow bill forward, looking neither left or right,
they eager to keep up, to stay in line.

Reflexively I braked, uncleated,
swung my leg over the crossbar,
clattered to the center of the road,
faced the traffic with outstretched arms,
both lanes, both ways,
and stood my ground.

And thus, under the gaze of all,
they passed and made their purposeful way.
She strode upon the far curb and waddled on,
all else bumped and leaped at the ledge,
the last one tumbled back, once, twice,

prevailed, and scurried to catch up
with flap of tiny wing.

Being Served

The plate that the kids ordered has come,
a pile of chicken fingers, fries upon fries,
a mono-hued clump of encrusted gold,
all crinkly, a platitude of food.

And here! here! my grilled Mediterranean fare,
a veggie jumble, jungle. Ah the consorting,
commingling shapes, the spectrum of it:
zucchini, squash, yellow peppers, red onions,
asparagus, and tomatoes, served on a bed
of basmati rice with a garden salad.

I gaze into it, take in the notes and strokes.
I hike my chair, unroll my fork.
I hear Debussy, see Monet, Renoir,
Cezanne, Degas.

From Haunts
of Coot and Hern

Under this gritty
high-traffic
four-lane city bridge,
gurgling through this culvert,
down this cement conduit,
this concave trough,
confined, channeled,
straight and steady,
Lord Alfred's babbling brook,
Roberts' flowery bonnie burn,
Gerard's wind-wandering,
weed-winding,
rollrock highroad,
roaring down
in coop and comb.*

* In coop and in comb: the convex and concave
'rib' effects of water running over stones
(Gerard Manley Hopkins, *Inversnaid*)

Upon Examination
of My One-Wood

Here in the dusty corner of the garage,
the leaning mildewed bag of my old sticks.
I pull out the driver as if to waggle it.
Look at that scuffed up, lifeless
wooden head, how small, petite, pathetic.
And that face I thought I knew,
how surprisingly thin, almost sleek,
the sweet-spot minuscule, a fairy
pinpoint between four tiny screws.

All, all is explained, revealed,
those near whiffs, those half-hearted
flights, the fifty yard fluffs,
the bladed sickening, scurrying,
skidding wonders.

All those years trudging the far fairways,
you and the others across my back,
clicking together at each step,
hope against hope, bogey unto bogey.

The discouragement, the repressed
anger, the splintered dreams.
I wasn't as bad as I thought,
only born too soon, set up to fail,
a victim of a manufactured flaw.

I see the laborer, the perpetrator,
in a shop in some old city:
Albany, Cincinnati, Milwaukee.
He has an apron and black mustache,
is carving, whittling, sanding,
polishing, lacquering.
He is honest, earnest, an unscientific
man proud of his product.
I can not blame him,
and time has soothed my wounds.

Sand

I stand amid the roar
Of a surf-tormented shore,
And I hold with my hand
Grains of the golden sand.
-- Edgar Allan Poe (A Dream Within a Dream)

You might not believe it when you've returned
from the beach and ended up with some
between your sheets, but we need more finely divided rock,
granules smaller than gravel and bigger than silt.
They must be angular, have fractured faces so as
to readily adhere to each other. We need them to make
roads, buildings, parking lots, runways, microchips,
wineglasses, cell-phone screens and artificial hips.
Filtration facilities and septic systems couldn't function
without them. Locomotives drop the sharp-sided
grains in front of their wheels to better stop.

The smooth rounded spherical stuff found in deserts
won't do, the winds have blown it about and worn it down,
it doesn't hold together. It's flighty, flimsy, you couldn't
build a decent sand castle out of it no matter how good
your bucket and shovel.
When you stand on it you sink right in up to your ankles.
That's good for beach volleyball and equestrian arenas
but not much else. The golf courses in Dubai
have had to fill their bunkers with hardy granules
imported from North Carolina. Balls hit into their own stuff

would poof right out of sight, there'd be no more fried-egg lies.

Blue

I've seen blue-eyed kittens, lots of bluejays,
caught glimpses of the blue of bluebirds in flight,
the iridescence of crows and doves when the light
was right. I've gotten good looks of bluebill ducks
through binoculars, watched them dive down,
waited and guessed where they might come up.
I've lived out West and seen blue mountains,
and lived back East amidst misty blue hills.
I've caught bluegills in hot weather,
seen blue shadows stretch out across snowy fields.
I've snorkeled and scubaed Australia's Great Barrier Reef,
seen thick schools of fish: solid blue, striped and spotted,
seen wondrous blue coral: sprigs and bulging brains of it.
I've gazed on especially blue skies in October,
and Blue Bells in late April or early May,
I've picked and savored blueberries,
stood on cliffs above deep blue lakes, inlets and coves,
sat next to campfires, smelled the blue smoke
and noted how it rose.
I've seen a lot of things that hint of blue:
stars, night lightening, water's mysterious florescence
are but a few.
I know I might not see some of these blues again,
that I won't be venturing out to meet a lot of new blues.
I've never seen blue whales, blue sharks,
blue footed boobies.
I hear that ice caves have marvelous blues,
are filled with both loud and soft spoken hues.

Competitive Freediver

Stilling his heart,
sipping the air,
he holds his breath
duck dives, descends,
a slim shadow
long fins slow waving,
down, down deep,
into the dead silence,
the beautiful black,
the crushing cold,
seeking calm,
comfort in fear.

All-Embracing Supplication

If I was a praying man, given to long prayers,
had friends and family standing or sitting
before a plentiful table, warm hands clasped,
I would pray for everyone, from those present
to the president, those holding high offices,
our representatives from both parties,
for the firefighters risking their lives out West,
policemen and policewoman who keep us safe,
for all those traveling, those who have lost loved ones,
for migrants fleeing persecution, those living
in violent cities, those in war torn countries,
for the astronauts up in space,
the minors and children trapped in caves,
the victims of volcanoes and earthquakes
whose homes have been destroyed,
for the blind and halt and lonely,
for the sick and elderly in nursing homes,
all those less fortunate than we.
I would ask for strength and guidance,
forgiveness, acceptance of whatever comes our way,
thanks for family and friends
and what we were about to receive.
And if I was honest, wholly openhearted,
in light of the afflictions I've recently known
others to have endured, or are enduring,
I would add that I'm truly thankful
for my good digestive track
and healthy bowel movements.

The Coming of the End Times --
Civilization As We Know It

It's appearing on the once smooth-faced young men,
on the up-and-coming square-jawed anchormen,
commentators, representatives of corporations
and products -- stubble, stubble, shadowy black
and silvery, bristling bold.
These men, these leaders, so carefully careless for now.
All they want is the hint of the casual, the relaxed look,
so they claim.

But I see trouble, an incipient bubbling disdain
for the civil act of daily shaving, for putting forth the effort,
for clean grooming. It loudly whispers of laziness,
shoddiness. It will not stop with penciled mustaches,
chin straps, goatees, soul patches, muttonchops
(friendly or otherwise).

Mark my words, it's a styleless slippery slope,
a slovenly passage to full beards, all out flowing,
frizzy, wild-eyed growth, to the Mountain Man,
Paleo Look. Soon enough collars and ties will go,
there will be t-shirts, tank tops, soiled bib jeans,
sandals, flip flops, bare feet -- calloused and grimy.

Precisely at Sunset

Some thirty odd years ago,
I sat on a boat in a southern clime
bathed in a calm golden sheen.
Liquid slow without a sound
the sun reached down,
the sea swelled up, a glowing
goblet was conceived,
the grandest I'd ever seen.

Smash-Mouth Pickleball

When I say I play pickleball,
they ask what is that.
I explain about the small courts and lowered nets,
the paddles and plastic balls,
the underhand serves and the dinking.
They smile and smile and think that's nice;
they see me at a community center for seniors,
standing about, conversing, tapping at the balls
that bounce my way, walking after those
which get by, that go between my legs
and roll to the bleachers.

I don't tell them I play with peering darting eyes,
await the slightest mistake, the fluffed shot,
a high ball to punish, to lash out at it
and make somebody pay.
My old gray coals have been stoked,
inside I glow again, feel the fire of youth.
I know the score all too well,
know this to be my last game, my last go,
and play with fiendish glee.

All the Marbles

In pickleball, when I'm ready to serve
for the last game, I like to call out,
"This one is for all the marbles."

At recess, I would get on my hands
and knees, knuckle down
with my bonker, my shooter,
tilt my head, hold my mouth just so,
steady my thumb.

I was good back then, in my prime.
We played for keeps. I owned, earned
a big cinched bag of them, cat-eyes,
aggies, swirls, steelies, clearies, comets.

Back in the classroom,
after the teacher past down the aisle,
my hand slid under the lid of my desk,
plunged in and let them roll through
my fingers, took in their cool
smooth roundness, and the soft
golden clicking sound.

Thrill Riding
and Graceful Dismounts

I've seen it in a lot of movies, but I've
never raced all out on a lathered steed.
I've never gone rawhide fast, held on
for dear life, felt the pounding rhythm,
been one with a beautiful beast.
I've never ridden down some canyon,
along some ridge, and reined him in,
came to a rearing stop, flew off
and landed cowboy light.

Many a time I got going as fast as possible
down the alley on my trusty Schwinn,
yahooing into the wind. I cut into
the backyard between the garage and garden,
my kickstand and fenders clattering.
I peddled full blast across the grass
to the back of the house, locked up
the coaster brake, skidded completely
around and vaulted free.

One Big Ass Sparkly Pinwheel

*Why should I be lonely,
is not our planet in the Milky Way?
-- Henry David Thoreau*

It's a thousand light years thick
and a hundred thousand light years in diameter,
made up of four-hundred billion stars,
some one-hundred billion planets.

I'm near the inner rim of the Orion Arm,
within the Lock Fluff of the Local Bubble,
in the Gould Belt.
That puts me about twenty-six thousand light years
from the center, which is a supermassive black hole
weighing four-and-a-half millions times as much as the
sun.

I'm whirling in a windless wind
at four-hundred-and-ninety thousand miles per hour;
even at that speed it will take a hundred and forty million
years to get all the way around.

And the whole kit and caboodle is flying off
through intergalactic space at six-hundred kilometers per
second, along with billions of other stickless pinwheels,
all sent flying away by one big bang that happened
13.7 billion years ago, give or take a billion.

When I step back and look at it from out there,

out there in the cold and black vacuum,
I get disoriented, can't tell up from down,
and see that this great toy of ours is just another speck.
I don't know that it makes me feel less lonely,
just smaller, more out of the way,
a little dizzy.

Upper Paleolithic Man

I would like to know the name of the guy
who, 30,000 odd years ago, painted the bison
on the Altamira ceiling, who crawled back in the cave
and held his marrow fat oil lamp up, decided were
to position his creations to take advantage
of the bumps and crevasses, decided to have some
of them standing and other lying down,
decided it would be worth the effort to do them
in polychrome: black, red brown and yellow.

I can see him working away: mixing the pigments
with his crude tools, climbing up, balancing things,
adding details to the painting that hadn't occurred
to him when he started.

What did they call him? Was he a Homo sapien
or Neanderthal? Maybe he was a woman?
Were the others impressed or did they think
he was a little cracked?
How many bothered to go look?

I wonder if when he got old, if he made it that far,
if he was able to make it back in and have a look,
and consider what he had done,
 and smile upon it.

Dunkirk

I saw the movie about a year ago.
There were a lot of dramatic events and scenes
but only one has stuck with me.
The stranded soldiers are enduring sporadic explosions,
rifle fire, and there appears to be no chance of escape.
Comrades have been dying, bodies washing up
on the beach, bumping into each other.
In the evening quiet, an unknown man is seen
in the distance, wading into the water, standing
for a moment, diving in, free-styling out with strong stroke.
He knows Dover's white cliffs are some 20 miles away,
he'll only get a little closer to home, the cold currents
will see to that.

I can see myself doing that, needing to escape --
and home being just over there.
I can see myself turning on my back and stroking,
using the moon as a guide, noting which phase
it's in -- finding it interesting that this particular one
is to be my last.
I probably would only make it a couple miles
before the fatigue and cold set in, before
the final panic, gasping and salty choking came.
Before that happened, I think I might find
some solace in the practiced movement.

ABOUT THE AUTHOR

I was born and raised in Saegertown, Pennsylvania. I received my B.S. and M.S. degrees in Physical Education from Slippery Rock State College (1969 and 1971), and my Ph.D. in Physical Education from The University of Iowa (1975). The lion's share of my teaching career was spent as a Professor of Physical Education at Eastern Washington University (1980-2012). I retired in 2012 and now live in Auburn, Alabama with my lovely wife Julie. I didn't start writing poetry until my retirement. My other serious hobbies are reading, swimming, bicycling, and painting. I have seized this publishing opportunity to have one of my paintings on the book cover. In case you would like to contact me about how wildly wonderful my poems are, my email is smelville27@gmail.com.

Made in United States
North Haven, CT
20 May 2025